D0050749

This book belongs to

....

(witch in training)

Spells
for
good times

Lauren White

MQP
MQ Publications Ltd

✧ CONTENTS ✧

· mortar and pestle.

chapter

How to use this book

How to use this book

If the rain is streaming down the windows,
you've just had a row with your best
friend or you're just plain fed-up, a
sprinkling of magic is just the thing to
bring out the sunshine!

All the spells in this book require everyday ingredients which should be easy to obtain.

Essential oils are a key ingredient in many spells. They are a potent distillation of the magical powers which many plants possess :

MINT	LAVENDER	ROSE	BERGAMOT
concentration	passion	relaxation	activity
clarity	purification	love	pleasure

Candles are also important. Don't use
scented candles; they often use synthetic
fragrance.
The color is very significant...

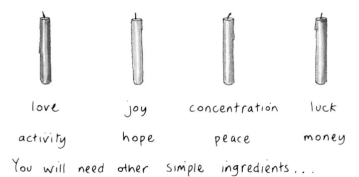

| love | joy | concentration | luck |
| activity | hope | peace | money |

You will need other simple ingredients...

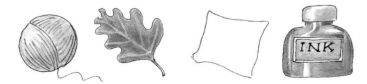

✧ THE SPELLS ✧

A brief description at the start of each spell will tell you, at a glance, its uses and applications.

There is also a key which gives a guide to the difficulty, reliability, and timing of each spell...

DIFFICULTY	TIME TAKEN	RELIABILITY
✳ ✳ ✳	✭	✭ ✭

DIFFICULTY				
	*			a piece of cake!
	*	*		no bother
	*	*	*	concentration required

TIME TAKEN				
	★			instant
	★	★		reserve the evening
	★	★	★	patience required...

RELIABILITY				
	★			good luck!
	★	★		tried and tested
	★	★	★	success guaranteed...

As you become more experienced you may want to
adapt or personalize some spells ~ or even devise
your own. Keep experimenting until you feel
completely happy with the results...

. Wand .

chapter

Experimenting with magic !

To experiment with magic, you will need the following:

(i) an open mind - be prepared to explore.

(ii) time - never perform magic in a hurry.

(iii) Space - you need to be able to arrange all of your tools and materials exactly how you want.

(iv) curiosity — experiment is the key to success.

(v) faith - belief in yourself and your magical powers is essential.

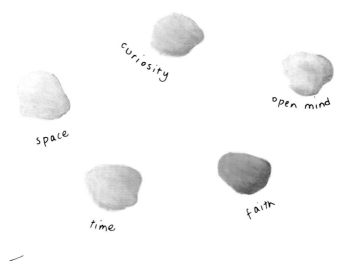

curiosity

open mind

space

time

faith

The rest is up to you...
Simply mix these ingredients, add a touch of serendipity and create your own bewitching masterpiece!

It's helpful to have a store of useful objects you're likely to need:

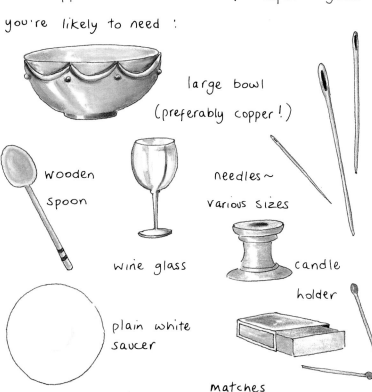

large bowl
(preferably copper!)

wooden spoon

wine glass

needles~
various sizes

candle holder

plain white saucer

matches

and, of course...

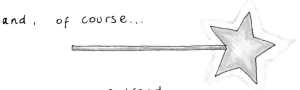

... a wand.

This isn't essential but it's a useful tool and a very personal object. You can make your own from wood, plastic, metal, anything you want.

The more you use your wand, the more special powers it gains . . .

lucky number

c h a p t e r

The only way is up !

THE BIG BANG!

If you are feeling a little bit "hopeless and unloved", this spell will shower positive feelings on you ~ transforming your state of mind.

DIFFICULTY	TIME TAKEN	RELIABILITY
*	★	★ ★ ★

The recipe here calls for marigold petals ~ you need "pot marigold" for this...

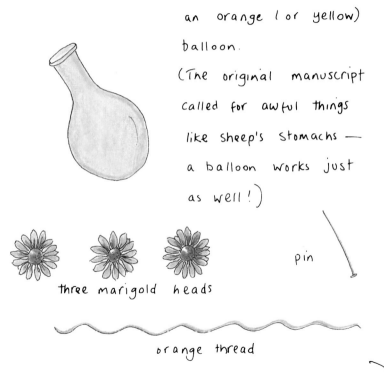

an orange (or yellow) balloon.
(The original manuscript called for awful things like sheep's stomachs — a balloon works just as well!)

pin

three marigold heads

orange thread

METHOD   (i) Pluck each petal carefully from the marigolds.

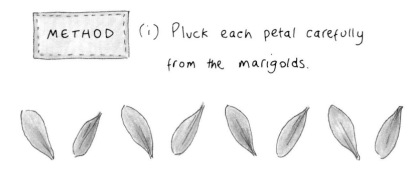

(ii) Gently "feed" them into the neck of the balloon.

(iii) Inflate the balloon.

NOTE   Take great care NOT to inhale any petals.

(iv) Suspend the balloon above your head.

(v) Close your eyes and, with the pin, pop
the balloon!

For the spell to work effectively, it's
essential to leave the petals where they fall.

RED HOT AND SIZZLING!

Some days you can feel cold and miserable all day long. Perform this ritual to conjure up warmth and energy.

DIFFICULTY	TIME TAKEN	RELIABILITY
*	⭐	⭐ ⭐ ⭐

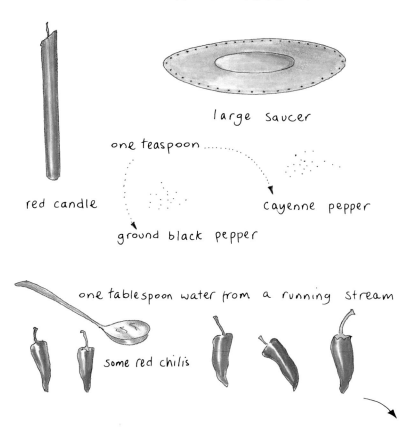

✿ YOU WILL NEED ✿

large saucer

red candle

one teaspoon

cayenne pepper

ground black pepper

one tablespoon water from a running stream

some red chilis

METHOD (i) Place the candle in the center of the saucer.

(ii) Arrange the chilis in a ring around it.

(iii) Pour the water around the base of the candle.

(iv) Sprinkle the ring of chilis with the two kinds of pepper.

(v) Light the candle.

(vi) Allow the candle to burn down.

As soon as the candle is lit, the atmostphere will be charged with fire and vigor. As it burns this will intensify...

IT'S A GIFT!

or

(the lucky horseshoe)

You can brighten up someone else's life with this spell. If you have a friend who could do with some luck, follow these instructions and you could change their life!

DIFFICULTY	TIME TAKEN	RELIABILITY
✶ ✶	✶ ✶ ✶	★ ★

✿ YOU WILL NEED ✿

Seven small envelopes

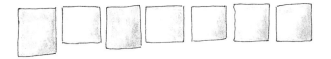

Seven pieces of paper

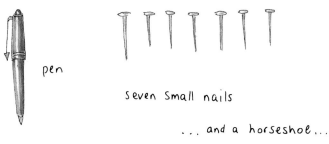

pen

Seven small nails

... and a horseshoe...

METHOD

(i) For seven days, each evening; write the name of your friend and something you wish for them on one of the pieces of paper.

⭐ SUGGESTIONS

health

love

luck

hope

money

(ii) Fold up the paper, pierce with the nail, and place in an envelope.

(iii) After seven nights...

Place the horseshoe on a mirrored surface and place the envelopes inside the "curve".

The horseshoe, a traditional symbol of good fortune, will add power to these "messages" and the mirror will reflect their energy outwards, and towards your friend...

...this will bring an immediate change of fortune...

NOTE

You can perform this spell for yourself, if you feel that you could do with a change of fortune, but the results can vary. Traditionally, it works best as a gift for a friend...

TO BURY BAD FEELINGS

DIFFICULTY	TIME TAKEN	RELIABILITY
*	* *	* * *

Moonphase -   Full moon

This spell will heal feelings of unhappiness or anger ~ perhaps after an argument or a bad experience ...

✫ YOU WILL NEED ✫

a large onion

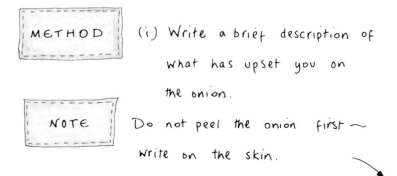

pen

METHOD   (i) Write a brief description of what has upset you on the onion.

NOTE   Do not peel the onion first — write on the skin.

· FOR EXAMPLE ·

Argument with my sister, over her
stealing my best shoes —— again.

(ii) Bury the onion somewhere secret.

(iii) Visualize the layers wasting away, one
by one.

Over the next few days, the problem will fade away...

Another way to rid yourself of unwanted feelings is to write them on a stone or pebble with a chalk.

Place the pebble in a fast-running stream and you will find that your troubles are simply "washed away"...

MAGIC BLANKET

If you are feeling tense and restless, and just can't settle, a cozy evening by the fire is the perfect way to relax, this spell will guarantee a warm atmosphere!

DIFFICULTY	TIME TAKEN	RELIABILITY
*	☆	☆ ☆

a cup of sage leaves ~
Sage is a powerful
"bad vibe buster!"

½ cup of pine needles

dried peel of
an orange

cinnamon stick

one dried, crushed chili pepper

METHOD (i) Crush all of the ingredients using a mortar and pestle.

(ii) Throw the mixture into the flames.

(iii) Gaze into the fire.

☆ At this point, you might want to say some personal words which are important to you...

As the flames crackle and spark
the air will be infused with a
sweet aroma and a magical
blanket of comfort will wrap
around your shoulders...

·fairy dust·

chapter

IV

Domestic bliss

HANDS-ON HELP

- ironing
- clean toilet
- bath dog
- weed garden
- complete tax return
- polish shoes
- do filing
- paint window

If your "to-do" list reads anything like this, you have two options:

a) Go to the cinema (!)

b) Perform this spell and attack the tasks
   in hand with gusto!

DIFFICULTY	TIME TAKEN	RELIABILITY
✳ ✳	✰	★ ★

✬ YOU WILL NEED ✬

red satin ribbon

bergamot oil

red candle

(i) Anoint the candle with oil.

(ii) Light the candle.

(iii) Tie one end of the ribbon to your left wrist,
the other to your right wrist.

(iv) Singe the ribbon over the flame, saying:

... Unbind me from my task ...

You will sizzle with energy and perform your jobs with astonishing speed!

CAUTION

Have water nearby, just in case !!!

IN THE GARDEN

It may suprise you , but most witches are extraordinarily good gardeners as they need to maintain a supply of fresh herbs for their potions.

You can test out your own magic " green fingers" with the following spells . . .

HOW TO MAKE A GARDEN TALISMAN

DIFFICULTY	TIME TAKEN	RELIABILITY
* *	✧ ✧	⭐ ⭐

✧ YOU WILL NEED ✧

oak leaf ~ the "father" of the forest

yellow ribbon ~ "sunshine"

small shell ~ "water"

ear of corn ~ "plenty"

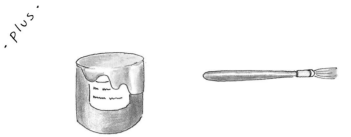

gold paint (or gold leaf if you're brave!)

⭐ Originally all the items would have been dipped in liquid gold ~ but this is probably impractical for you...

METHOD (i) "Gild" each item.

(ii) When the ear of corn, the oak leaf, and

the shell are dry, make a small hole in the shell and tie them all together with the yellow ribbon.

(iii) Hang the talisman in your garden.

This represents all the ingredients you need for a healthy garden.

A SPELL TO "BLESS" THE GARDEN

DIFFICULTY	TIME TAKEN	RELIABILITY
✳	☆ ☆	★ ★ ★

✫ YOU WILL NEED ✫

compass

four white pebbles

pen or paint

METHOD

(i) Choose four simple words which will form your own personal "blessing".

(ii) Write one word on each pebble.

(iii) At sunrise "plant" one pebble at each compass point in the garden.

may my garden grow

· Repeat each spring ·

THE GOOD COOK'S SECRET WEAPON!

If your cakes collapse, souffles sink, rissoles revolt, you need a sprinkling of culinary magic. Transform your cooking!

DIFFICULTY	TIME TAKEN	RELIABILITY
* * *	☆ ☆	☆

☆ YOU WILL NEED ☆

basic small cooking utensils

clean white dish towel

teaspoon sugar ~ for sweetness

large bowl of cold spring water

teaspoon salt ~ for flavor

drop of peppermint oil ~ for a fresh, light touch

white candle

 METHOD

(i) Lay out the dish towel

(ii) Place the utensils on it, in a ring and place the candle in the center and light it.

(iii) Add the peppermint oil, salt, and sugar to the water.

(iv Immerse your hands in the water and feel them gaining strength, sensitivity, and lightness of touch...

(v) Place your hands on either side of the candle and blow it out.

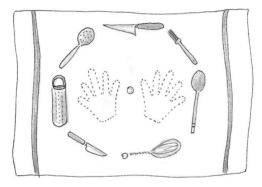

(vi) Remove the utensils and candle, roll up your sleeves, shake the dish towel, and set to work!

·lucky charm·

chapter

All in the mind

PSYCHIC CLEAN-UP!

If you are feeling mentally "over-cooked", this spell will clear out all the debris and cool your fevered brow!

DIFFICULTY	TIME TAKEN	RELIABILITY
*	⭐	⭐ ⭐ ⭐

☆ YOU WILL NEED ☆

teaspoon

Some detergent
(washing up liquid)

small bowl

length of wire

Essential oil of: spearmint - concentration

lavender - purification

lemon - cleansing

(two drops of each)

hat pin (or similar item)   a little warm water

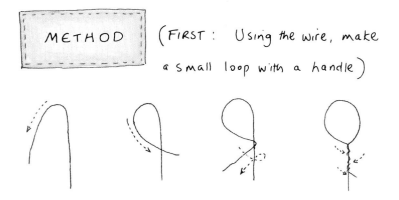

METHOD

(FIRST: Using the wire, make a small loop with a handle)

(i) Put three teaspoons of water in the bowl and add two teaspoons of detergent.

(ii) Add the oils and gently stir.

(iii) Sit quietly and reflect on your negative thoughts.

(iv) Dip the wire in the mixture and "breathe" these thoughts out into bubbles...

(v) As they float down, pop each one!

NOTE You MUST pop each bubble before it hits the ground.

Your worries will be gone.

ZING POTION!

.... To "kick-start" a sluggish day...

DIFFICULTY	TIME TAKEN	RELIABILITY
*	⭐	⭐ ⭐

NOTE

This spell requires a
favorite cup or
mug. The more spells
you perform using it,
the more magical
energy it will retain...

✿ YOU WILL NEED ✿

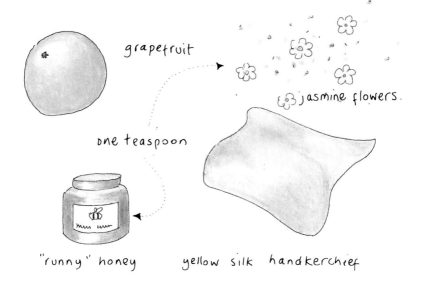

grapefruit

jasmine flowers.

one teaspoon

"runny" honey

yellow silk handkerchief

METHOD

(i) Squeeze the juice of the grapefruit into a cup.

(ii) Put the spoonful of honey and the jasmine flowers in the cup, then ~

⇒ JUST ADD HOT WATER ⇐

(iii) Wait for three minutes then strain the liquid through the silk handkerchief.

(iv) Pour into your 'best' cup and drink the elixir, facing the rising sun.

You will feel energised, enthusiastic, and full of "zing" all day long!

SWEET DREAMS

This is a recipe for a special protective powder to place under your pillow. It is said to encourage sleep and beautiful dreams ~ AND to make those dreams come true!

DIFFICULTY	TIME TAKEN	RELIABILITY
✶	✩ ✩ ✩	★ ★

✩ YOU WILL NEED ✩

gold pouch or envelope

½ teaspoon :

basil powder

dried spearmint leaves

grated nutmeg

small gold charm

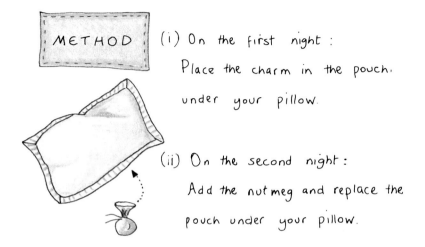

METHOD

(i) On the first night :
Place the charm in the pouch,
under your pillow.

(ii) On the second night :
Add the nutmeg and replace the
pouch under your pillow.

(iii) On the third night : follow the same procedure
with the spearmint.

(iv) On the fourth night, do the same with the
basil powder.

From the fifth night onwards you
will sleep soundly, dream sweetly,
and wake up feeling glorious!

EFFERVESCENCE!

To obtain inspiration, verve, and mental energy, perform this simple spell.

DIFFICULTY	TIME TAKEN	RELIABILITY
*	★	★ ★ ★

YOU WILL NEED

large beautiful bowl

½ cup white vinegar

teaspoon baking powder

glitter or tiny fragments of foil

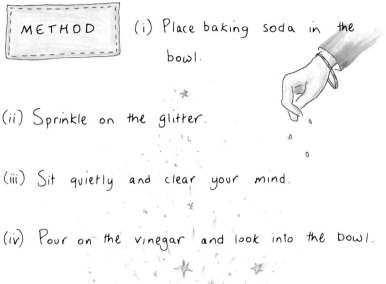

| METHOD | (i) Place baking soda in the bowl. |

(ii) Sprinkle on the glitter.

(iii) Sit quietly and clear your mind.

(iv) Pour on the vinegar and look into the bowl.

As if by magic (!), your mind will fizzle with new ideas...

NEW SHOES

or

the transformation spell

This spell provides the "tired old you" with a sense of change.

Its perfect if you want to make changes to:

your job . . . . . .

your home . . . . .

your boyfriend . . . .

. . . . . your life . . . . . .

It symbolizes leaving the old and welcoming the new.

DIFFICULTY	TIME TAKEN	RELIABILITY
✳ ✳	⭐ ☆	⭐ ⭐

 new moon

MOONPHASE

Perform this spell in a place which is special to you ～ your garden, for instance, or a wood where you like walking, or a quiet beach...

old shoes

new shoes

stick of chalk

METHOD (i) wear your old shoes.

(ii) Draw a chalk line on the ground and place your new shoes on one side of it.

(If you're on the beach, just make an 'indent' in the sand)

(iv) Stand on the other side of the line.

(v) Remove your shoes and jump over the line.

(vi) Put on your new shoes and say "goodbye".

NOTE

It is desirable to burn your old shoes and scatter the ashes— you might even like to hold a "service" for them to say a final farewell...

. full moon .

chapter

VI

Getting it together

TO SUMMON FRIENDS

This simple spell will attract visitors to your door.

DIFFICULTY	TIME TAKEN	RELIABILITY
* *	☆	★ ★

This spell is based on the powerful effects that grapes and grape seeds have to attract. They are an ancient symbol of hospitality and a warm welcome.

A red cloth (preferably velvet)

a glass of
white wine

handful of basil leaves
(cheery and positive)

one teaspoon rosemary
(activity)

bucket of
spring water

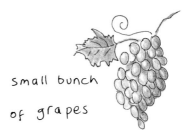

small bunch
of grapes

·plus·

METHOD

(i) Add the wine to the
bucket of water.

(ii) Crush the basil and rosemary and add
them to the liquid.

(iii) Immerse the cloth in the liquid
and "wash" your door!

(iv) Eat the grapes but save the pips.

(v) Sprinkle these along your doorstep.

Perform this spell and people won't be able to stop themselves from knocking at your door...

TABLE SETTING

If you want your dinner party to go with a swing but have visions of bickering, or even worse, bored guests blearily looking at their watches (!), this is a way to inject some magical "bon homie"...

DIFFICULTY	TIME TAKEN	RELIABILITY
✱ ✱	★ ★	★ ★

YOU WILL NEED

blue candle ~
for harmony and peace

Ivy

handful of camomile
flowers

METHOD   (i) Prepare the table well in advance.

(ii) Weave a garland from the ivy.

NOTE (i)   This represents evergreen friendship and close connection.

(iii) Place the candle in the center of the table surrounded by the ivy wreath.

(iv) Strew the camomile flowers (see note (ii) around the wreath.

(v) Light the candle and allow it to burn down completely.

NOTE (ii) Camomile flowers create a soothing relaxing atmosphere.

You might like to use some to make a tea to drink as the candle burns...

Just before guests arrive...

Pluck four leaves from the ivy wreath and place one at each corner of the table under the tablecloth. If this is impractical perhaps you could attach them to the underneath of the table top...

Result? ..

A cordial warm occasion that
you can relax and enjoy...

CELEBRATION SPELL

This is the perfect spell to make a wedding or birthday into a sparkling occasion.

DIFFICULTY	TIME TAKEN	RELIABILITY
* *	★ ★ ★	☆☆☆

champagne cork

small rose quartz crystal

copper wire to transfer positive energy

red candle

sharp knife

champagne or white wine

Before the event ~

METHOD (i) Light the candle.

(ii) Cut the cork down the middle and hollow out a small piece of each half.

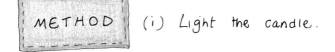

(iii) Place the crystal inside.

(iv) Bind the two halves together with copper wire.

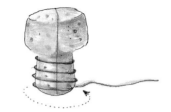

(v) By moonlight, float the cork in the glass of champagne.

During the event ~

Place the cork somewhere secret, near to the guest(s) of honor. They will glow with pleasure throughout the day...

· magic toadstool ·

chapter

VII

Emergency spells ~ if all else fails!

HOW NOT TO GAIN WEIGHT

There's a gallon of ice cream in the refrigerator, a chocolate bar in the cupboard, and the cookie jar is full.

Go on—indulge yourself!

(just do this spell first)

☆ YOU WILL NEED ☆

a length of fine white thread

a photograph of yourself

foil

METHOD

FIRST ~ You will need to measure your waist and take some thread <u>exactly</u> the same length.

✩ You can avoid the "measuring bit" by simply pulling the thread around your waist and cutting to the appropriate length.

(i) Tie a knot in the centre of the thread.

(ii) Place this, with your photograph, in the

foil and wrap tightly.

(iii) Place under a heavy object.

(iv) "Bon Appetit!"

NOTE This spell lasts for 24 hours only,
in any lunar cycle, so, sadly it is
not the ultimate super·slim·spell
~ that's another book!

MAKING A MAGICAL WATER

☆ YOU WILL NEED ☆

the, finely chopped, peel of
an orange ~ for love

a handful of fresh, white
rose petals ~ for purity

one teaspoon thyme leaves ~
for luck

½ teaspoon dried ginger
~ for wealth

Mix all of the ingredients together in a beautiful china bowl.

Add one pint of fresh spring water
(Use your wand to stir, if you have one)

Anoint :

coins ...   clothes ...   cars ...   OR

wash your hands, if you feel stressed.

NOTE This is a handy stand-by, but it MUST
be made fresh, it cannot be stored...

WISH LIST !

To make your heart's desire a reality...

YOU WILL NEED

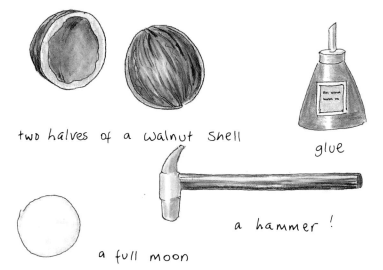

two halves of a walnut shell

glue

a hammer !

a full moon

METHOD (i) Whisper your "wish" into the walnut shell and immediately seal the two halves together.

NEXT FULL MOON :

(ii) Go to a secret place.

NOTE
You can only use ONE wish!

(iii) Take the hammer, and with one clean stroke, smash open the shell to release your wish into the night air....

During the next twelve months, your wish will come true.

" RESCUE "

A cure for feeling downcast, crotchety, and crusty !

a big dose of happiness !

If you feel like there is a very large black cloud following you wherever you go, there is something you can do !

This spell uses roses which have great magical powers, they help to sooth a troubled soul and bring hope ...

glass jar ~ this must be
sterilized

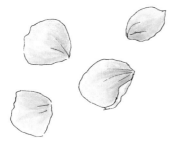

enough yellow rose
petals to fill the
jar

a ring

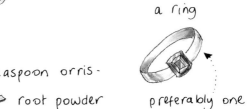

teaspoon orris-
root powder

(to "fix" the spell)

preferably one
that you wear often

METHOD

(i) Take your favorite ring, wash it under running water and place it in the jar.

☆ Running water will "cleanse" the ring of any negative energy.

(ii) Cover with rose petals and replace the lid.

(iii) Place on your windowsill in full bright moonlight, leave overnight.

(iv) In the morning, place the ring on your finger and troubled thoughts will simply float away . . .

About the Author

"Adding a sprinkling of magic to the everyday" perfectly describes Lauren's original style of drawing. This is precisely what she does in her little books of spells.

Lauren lives in the Bedfordshire village of Cranfield where her family have lived for generations, although she studied fine art in Hull and London and worked as a wildlife illustrator before returning to the village. She shares, what she describes as, her "crumbling cottage" with her partner Michael and her "familiar", a little black dog called Jack. This is where she brews up her own spells and potions (of the gentlest kind…), plays the piano and stops the garden invading the house!

Lauren loves drawing and always has a sketchbook in her pocket. As well as her books of spells, Lauren has produced a series of six little gift books celebrating the simple things in life for MQ Publications. Her designs for Hotchpotch greetings cards are sold around the world.

Published by MQ Publications Limited
12 the Ivories 6-8 Northampton Street London N1 2HY
email: mail@mqpublications.com

ISBN: 1-84072-128-6

3 5 7 9 0 8 6 4

Printed in China